FLAT SPOT

The Seven Mistakes Entrepreneurs Make That Put The Brakes on Growth

Gavin Preston

First published in Great Britain in 2012 by 90 Day Books, a trading name of
Meaningful Goals Ltd., Sussex, England.
www.90daybooks.com

Edited by Lis Clegg and Kevin Bermingham, 90 Day Books

Cover design by Gary Prince Design Ltd. www.garyprincedesign.co.uk

Author's cover photograph by John Cassidy www.johncassidyheadshots.com

British Library Cataloguing in Publication Data.
A catalogue record for this book is available from the British Library.

V1-Pocket Edition
ISBN 978-1-908101-24-2

1. Business & Economics

ACKNOWLEDGEMENTS

This book is dedicated to my parents. If my father, Harold, had not passed me a book at the age of 15 called *The Success System That Never Fails* by W. Clement Stone my fascination with peak performance and business may have never been born. His constant belief, motivation and support is of great value to me. My mother's friendship, love, dedication and work ethic has been a great role model with wonderful encouragement and unwavering support.

Special thanks to my brother Craig. The mark of a person is in their deeds, not their words. If ever I was in a fix with only the one phone call I could make, it would be to him.

And thanks to my clients. You have, and continue to be, my greatest teachers. I am grateful to share this journey of exploration and growth with you. Your successes inspire me further.

Testimonials

"Starting a business is easy - anyone can do that. Growing a business is hard - and Gavin knows exactly how to do that. Read his insights, follow his plan and take action - do those three things and your business will grow, it is inevitable."

David Taylor, Author of the Naked Leader series, Professor of Leadership at Warwick University Business School and Business Ambassador for The Prince's Trust."

"Gavin is a fantastic, inspirational coach who really took time to understand me as a person and challenged me to think about my business in a very different way. This has made a huge difference to the way I think and run my business every day. I genuinely believe that his involvement over the last 12 months has made me grow and develop in a way beyond what I believed was possible."

Jill Hague, Area Commercial Director, HSBC

CONTENTS

INTRODUCTION

"If I had one hour to save the world, I would spend 55 minutes defining the problem and only five minutes finding the solution."

Albert Einstein

Does the following scenario strike a chord with you?

You have been running your business for a number of years. You have seen success. Revenues and profits have increased for a number of years, as has the size of your workforce and the complexity of your business. Whilst it has probably been hard work, you have no doubt been fuelled by adrenalin, by the buzz that you get from success.

Maybe your business is smaller and you have hit a plateau, a flat spot in your growth, because there is only so much you can do and you need to find a way to scale your business.

However, if you lift your head from the daily treadmill for a minute you notice some things are not the same as they used to be. You are running harder and harder and getting nowhere. The strategies that delivered growth in the past are delivering at best meagre growth, if any at all. Hiccups in the delivery of your business appear to take on their own life as fully-fledged problems, or fires that need your attention to be put out. Increasingly you are getting dragged into the day-to-day noise of running the business with little time to stand back and look at where the business is heading. Your employees are disengaged and morale is low. They question why you need to grow the business any further: "Surely we are doing OK as we are?" Revenues have flattened and you have faced increasing costs of doing your business. Energy costs, distribution and travel costs and raw material prices have all gone up. Margins have been squeezed and profits are suffering as a result. Cashflow is tight and there is little leeway being granted by your bank.

The buzz you used to get from your thriving company has been replaced by fatigue. Your confidence has been dented and you continually ask yourself the questions "Why is this not working like it used to?" "What am I / we doing wrong?" "What is the best thing to do to turn this around?" and the big one: "Am I good enough to get this company back into growth?" These questions are wearing you down.

You have hit a flat spot in your business. In motor racing a flat spot is *"the term given to the area of a tyre that is worn heavily on one spot after a moment of extreme braking or in the course of a spin. This ruins its handling, often causing severe vibration, and may force a driver to pit for a replacement set of tyres"* (definition from the official Formula 1 website).

It's time for a pit stop

You know you need to do something differently, but you don't know where to start looking for the cause of the situation, let alone a solution.

Who do you turn to for a sounding board, for help in identifying the things that need to change in your company, for help in delivering a solution, for a strategy to accelerate growth in your business?

This book is meant to give you that pit stop before a fresh start. It puts the spotlight on some key areas of your business that may be off the pace. It highlights seven mistakes that entrepreneurs and business owners make in their business that put the brakes on growth and gives key tips towards doing something about it.

If the most important part of problem solving is recognizing that you have a problem and being clear on what the problem is, then this book will serve you well. It will highlight key areas to improve in your business.

In my book *Formula Won for Business,* I take you through the strategies to address these problems and The Formula for accelerating growth in your business: *P A C E*.

CHAPTER 1: NO PURPOSE (NO 'WHY')

"Being the richest man in the cemetery doesn't matter to me... Going to bed at night saying we've done something wonderful... that's what matters to me."

Steve Jobs, Apple

Current Question a business owner may ask:
How do we increase our sales and profit?

I see many companies and the people within them lose sight of what they are about, what they are up to in their market and in the world. Over time this erodes the drive in an organisation, the vibrancy of spirit that unleashes creativity, perseverance, growth and pace.

Each year they focus inward, on themselves. Attention is firmly on growing their revenues and profit, often with a short-term focus. This is particularly so with companies with demanding external stakeholders, companies responding to the demands of their investors or bankers. In some cases, the short-term, profit-maximising strategies erode the lifetime value of customers to that business and have a negative impact on brand reputation.

The leaders or managers in the business are set budgets and growth targets and told to get on with achieving them. All the focus becomes about wringing every last bit of revenue out of existing customers and winning new business in order to hit those targets. Those that lead the business drive their people harder and yet the lack of engagement by the individuals charged with increasing sales, increasing productivity and expanding into new markets can be seen in their lukewarm response to the increased pressure from above.

A cycle of growing frustration can ensue. The company leadership wonders why some of the customer-facing sales staff are not hitting targets and customer satisfaction falls while customer attrition increases. They cannot understand why workforce productivity is plateauing and why the employees are complaining about the pressure they are being put under to hit growth targets. To address that, senior management of the company manage the performance of the sales staff with a bigger stick in attempt to force engagement and sales performance. Employees are increasingly frustrated by the heavy-handed management style and feel badly done to, and in the worst cases, feel beaten up.

I have observed something: the bigger the stick wielded by management, the more employees appear to become anaesthetised to the pain. The focus, for some, moves from achieving the target and onto doing just enough to avoid the worst of the beating, onto doing just enough to keep their head below the parapet.

I see more and more 'punch drunk' employees wondering: "What is it (the pressure of work) all about?" This is more prevalent where you have a growing proportion of the workforce being Generation Y (those born in the mid-1980s) and now in their 20s who don't live to work, they work to live. They want something more from their lives, more from their work than hitting a 'meaningless' target. They want to be engaged with something of meaning.

If the lacklustre morale and performance in-house is not enough to contend with, some customers start to sense a shift in their own experience with the business. The delicate balance between a customer feeling served and valued and them feeling sold to and 'just another sale' starts to tip the wrong way in the eyes of the customer.

This is not a formula for accelerated and sustained growth. It is a formula for forced and short-lived incremental growth, employee disengagement and customer attrition.

One medium-sized business I worked with set their divisional Managing Directors' sales targets for the year based upon the revenues required to cover their cost base plus a certain profit margin. The business owner was getting frustrated that some of the divisions were not breaking even and was getting increasingly impatient at the apparent lack of capability of the Divisional Managing Directors and their sales team. When I spoke to the owner about the need for a clear goal and direction as to where the group of companies was heading, for a strategy to get there, his response was: "What is the point of that if they can't break even? All they have to do is sell!"

In reality there was no clear direction for the business. With competing brands under the same roof and no clear market positioning there was no strategy for growth. The budgets that were set were meaningless to the people charged with achieving them. Morale was low, performance was average and the call from the management team was that they needed leadership and a clear vision of where the group of companies was heading from the business owner.

Targets set need to have meaning and a purpose.

Of course there has to be a focus on revenue and profit growth. Setting targets and measuring our performance against those targets is essential to good performance. You will have no doubt heard that often-used management phrase: "What gets measured, gets done".

If we look to nature for a moment, there are a lot of parallels between life (including business) and nature. In nature everything is either growing or dying. There are momentary pauses between the tide coming in and going out, between the changing seasons, between night and day, but there is always movement; change that follows a cycle. In business and the economy we see cycles. Human beings are programmed to learn and to grow. We are at our happiest when we are learning, when we are taking on a challenge, when we are growing. Some people find their need for a challenge in business / their career, others through sport, others through being a fantastic parent or friend. When there is no challenge, no growth, that is when we lose our drive and fulfilment. Over time dissatisfaction and ambivalence start to build.

As in nature, you either grow or die.

Therefore it is essential that we focus on and deliver growth in the company.

Of course we need to focus on growth. My point is that I have seen many times, in SMEs and in corporates, employees and their managers losing sight of why they are striving for those targets other than to hit an arbitrary budget. The focus becomes entirely on the money instead of who they are serving. The focus is on short-term profit maximisation instead of the value they add to their customers, instead of the difference their product or service makes.

Apple focused on making insanely great products. That was their purpose and also, as Steve Jobs famously said, "To make a dent in the Universe". At times that vision was at odds with short-term profit maximisation.

I believe that in order to accelerate performance in a company in a sustainable way the business needs a bigger purpose, a bigger why.

At the time of writing Apple were the largest company in the world by market capitalisation.

The Bigger the Why, The Easier the How

In my book *Formula Won for Business* I take you through my five-step process (**S T A R T**) for getting you on the grid and creating a powerful and engaging purpose in your business.

Tip for the Top

- **Ask a better Question:**

  What is our bigger Why?

  What is it that we are 'up to' in the world?

  Who are we really serving?

  If there was a bigger impact we could have
  for our customers / in our market place,
  what would it be?

- **Identify your bigger why**

CHAPTER 2: WRONG THINKING / MINDSET (WRONG 'WHO')

"You cannot solve a problem with the same class of thinking that got you here in the first place."

Albert Einstein

Current Question a business owner may ask:

"What is going wrong in this company?"

"Am I good enough to get this company back into growth?"

When we read about businesses that succeed, we read about their strategies, about their innovative products or services and about the entrepreneurs or leaders at the helm. Those at the helm are described as charismatic, inspirational, dynamic, demanding and even maverick. Much is written about the kind of business leaders they are and the often audacious moves they make. It is often implied that such entrepreneurs were born with that talent.

Much less attention is given to what goes on behind the scenes, and I don't just mean behind closed doors of the company. I mean what goes on behind the eyes of those at the helm of a successful business.

Some thought leaders believe what we are experiencing in our business and in our lives today is a direct result of what we were focusing on and thinking about in the past. What we focus on and think about in the present will determine what we experience in the future.

THOUGHTS ➡ ACTIONS ➡ RESULTS

As human beings we are creatures of habit. Most of our day-to-day behaviour / actions are automatic. They are habitual. Right from the moment we open our eyes in the morning we start our daily routines on automatic pilot.

For many, the start of every day follows the same order. They follow the same routine for getting ready in the morning, eating the same breakfast, travelling the same route to work and sitting behind the same desk before going into the same weekly meetings in the same meeting room with everyone sat in the same chairs week on week.

"The definition of insanity is doing the same thing over and over and expecting different results".

Benjamin Franklin

You have got your business to its current stage as a result of your thinking and actions of the past. If your business performance has been plateauing then you are going to have to think differently about your business. You are going to have to take different actions, review and possibly change your strategy, raise your game in terms of the way you lead your employees and engage with customers and prospective customers. This requires you to change. I can help you with that.

We may intellectually recognize that by keeping on doing the same things we will keep getting the same result. However, there is a big difference between common sense and common practice. Given that most of our behaviours and the thoughts that precede them are habitual, often completely unconscious, it is not hard to see why we often hear the phrase "a leopard never changes its spots" or "they tried to change but then they just reverted to type".

If we are going to learn from Einstein then we need to change our thinking. In order to accelerate performance in a business, the people at the helm of the business need to think differently. They then need to get the people who work with them in the business to think differently. It starts at the top.

You need to think differently.

Change the thinking of the business owner and change the example they set. Change the thinking of the business owner and change the results they get.

Few people actually change their thinking and the resulting behaviour. The *American Heart Journal* published the results of a study in which they evaluated more than 1,200 men and women who were overweight and had suffered a heart attack. In the 12 months following their heart attack, participants of the study had lost a mere 0.2% of their body weight. What is surprising is that even the prospect of an early death was not enough to cause the patients to change their unhealthy lifestyle choices. That study is one of a number that demonstrate the small number of people that actually change their thinking and therefore their behaviour even when faced with a life-or-death scenario.

Some would argue that behavioural change does not work and that people revert to type. In my opinion it is more that people revert to their most-practised behaviour rather than revert to type. Therefore, if we are going to change our thought patterns and our behaviour we have to persevere and practise them until they become the new most-practised behaviour.

I have observed there are a number of factors that get in the way of persevering with the new ways of thinking and resultant behaviours:

Insufficient Reasons

Individuals may say that they want to change but they don't make change a must. They do not have enough reasons why changing their behaviour is important to them and is an absolute must, and why it is a must right now.

Reach the limit of your old identity

Our identity is the way we see ourselves.

I will illustrate this point using a well-known example: lottery winners. We have all heard of stories of people from a low-income background winning several million pounds on the lottery and then a few years later they are often worse off than they were before they won the money. One explanation for this is that their identity (the way they saw themselves) was being of low income, living a certain lifestyle and with a particular set of friends. When they won the lottery, the reality was very different to the kind of person they saw themselves as. The subconscious mind will go to great lengths to bring the 'external world' in line with their deeply ingrained 'internal world'. Whether it be through a spending spree, unsuccessful investments, family gifts or other means, actions were taken that resulted in the external world being re-aligned with the internal world.

I am not suggesting that you would fritter your money away like the aforementioned lottery winners. The point I make is that entrepreneurs can only take their business as far as their thinking, as far as their identity will allow. An entrepreneur running a £500,000 revenue business has a different identity (sees themselves differently) to one running a £20 million revenue business. An entrepreneur running a £100 million business has a different identity to one running a £2 million business. If you are going to take your business into the next phase of growth, adopt an identity in line with the size of business you want.

Inconsistency

To change your mindset, you have to practise the new way of thinking with consistency and discipline in order that it becomes the most practised behaviour, in order that it becomes habit.

For those who decide they are going to make changes, many will start off with great promise. They will, for example, start to see themselves as an entrepreneur running a successful £40 million business and visualise this outcome on a daily basis. They might start taking the necessary steps to make this happen in their business. Then after a few weeks, sometimes less, they become increasingly inconsistent in taking the necessary steps to grow the business and in their mindset conditioning.

A hallmark of those at the top of their game is discipline and consistency.

Visualising the wrong scenarios

The power of the mind is phenomenal. The subconscious mind does not know the difference between what we vividly imagine and reality. It will then go to great lengths to create in reality what we spend time vividly imagining.

Athletes have long been practising visualisation to improve their performance. They spend time imagining the race in their mind's eye and seeing the outcome they want. They are literally programming their own body and nervous system to deliver the performance they want.

The mistake most people make is that not only do they not spend time visualising the results they want to achieve but, worse than that, they spend the time programming in the worse-case scenario. Without necessarily being conscious of it, they spend time thinking about what could go wrong and imagine the worst-case scenarios. We call that worry. Remember, the brain does not know the difference between what you vividly imagine and reality.

They don't get back up

Success leaves behind it a trail of clues. One such clue is that successful people in business, sport, the arts and other endeavours are persistent. They have great resilience and can pick themselves up after a setback, dust themselves off and keep going for their objective.

All too often, I see business people with a great idea and a viable strategy get floored by a setback. Whether that was key pieces of business that fell through, a debt that turned bad, their banker changing the goal posts or falling profits; I see it knocking the confidence of business leaders.

During challenging economic conditions we see many business owners working harder and harder only to stand still. With business performance worsening or losses building for a number of years, I have seen entrepreneurs losing their spark and in some cases questioning whether to continue. Their mindset becomes defeatist and negative and this impacts on the decisions they take, on the way they interact with customers and employees and creates a downward spiral in terms of results.

Too many people give up. Often, unbeknown to them, right before the breakthrough.

In my book *Formula Won for Business*, I take you through my mindset-tuning strategy – **R A C E R**

Tip for the Top

- **Ask a better Question:**

  "What do leading entrepreneurs spend their time thinking about?"

  "What are the beliefs and mindset of leading entrepreneurs and how can I focus my thinking in the same way?"

- **To accelerate the performance of your business, you need to think differently. Get the inner game right and the outer game will follow.**

- **Who do you need to become to take your business to the next level?**

Chapter 3: No Strategic Edge (No 'how')

> **Current Question a business owner may ask:**
>
> "How do we do more of the same?"
>
> "How do we increase sales?"

Lack of Clarity on the End Game

Everyone in the organisation needs to clearly understand the goals they are aiming for and the part they play in achieving the overall company vision.

If you take a look under the bonnet of a business that is struggling you will find a lack of clarity on the goals of the organisation with fuzzy or no objectives for the employees. There is often no overall vision of what the business is aiming for, let alone passion and drive to move at any pace.

Inwardly Focused

In my experience, a lot of businesses have their heads down working and they are very introspective. It is almost as if they go about the world with their eyes closed to what is going on around them. They compare their performance against internally set budgets, they compare their performance against how they did last year. One division or region compares its performance against another. They do not spend enough time looking out at the external market place to see whether they are taking the right steps to stay ahead and grow the business not only now, but in two, five, ten years' time.

Whilst comparing your performance against last year's or that of another office / branch / region of your business can drive incremental improvement, it is not a meaningful comparison for accelerated growth.

I have worked with a number of organisations that consistently measure progress against each other and against last year. Measuring performance against targets and against other areas of the business ensures a competitive focus and does drive performance improvement, but there is a risk.

As a business, you could be demonstrating year-on-year growth but because you are so inwardly focused you are not paying attention to the changes taking place in the market place, changes in customer needs / wants and how customers are responding to what your competitors are up to. Customers do not look at your performance last year and continue to buy your product and service if you have made incremental improvements when there is a significantly better solution being offered by another company. This is a lesson that Nokia all too painfully experienced in 2009-2011. They did not respond to the market move towards smart phones anywhere near quick enough. In the short term they still posted healthy sales volumes off the back of sales of their traditional mobile phones to developing countries. That, however, is only ever shortlived.

As technology moves on and customers demand more, it is crucial you actively watch where the market is moving and either try to predict where it is going or at least keep up with it.

In the busy day-to-day operation of a company, there is plenty to keep us occupied. Business has to be won; product or service prepared or manufactured and then delivered; staff have to be led, managed and all too often performance managed; key stakeholders have to be kept engaged and cashflow has to be managed carefully. Running a complex business, the days pass in a blur of meetings and dealing with the pressing issues of the moment. There is little time to spend looking at what other players in your marketplace are up to, never mind what are the trends affecting other industries. However, you cannot afford not to.

A key mistake business leaders make is not taking a look at the world around them and spotting the key trends that are taking place that affect their industry and business.

No Strategic Edge

The next mistake made, leading on from the lack of awareness of key trends in the marketplace and moves competitors are making, is proceeding without a strategy that gives you an edge.

There are many companies that follow a 'me too' strategy of copying what an established player in the market place is doing. The problem with this is there is nothing about them that stands out, apart from being a poor copy. There is nothing that differentiates them in the eyes of the customer. In a crowded market place, customers will make a buying decision based on criteria that are important to them, e.g. product or service quality, price, customer service or what the brand stands for.

In order to accelerate growth in your business you need a clearly defined route to get you to your end game. A strategy that sets you apart from the competition and gets you to stand out in the eyes of your customer for all of the right reasons.

In my book *Formula Won for Business* I take you through my **S A T N A V** process to direct you to your Strategic Edge.

Tip for the Top

- **Ask A Better Question:**

  "What are the key trends in the world that will affect your business in the next five – ten years and what are you doing today to take advantage of them and lead the market?"

  "What strategies would differentiate you in the market place and accelerate growth?"

- **Actively select a strategy that will take you from where you are now to where you want to get to.**

Chapter 4: Inadequate Capability (No 'how')

> **Current Question a business owner may ask:**
> "How do we put this fire out?"

A key characteristic of businesses with sustained growth is that a large proportion of their employees are talented and motivated. Highly skilled people who are hungry to perform at their best are an acceleration force in any business.

If you have an organisation that is showing poor performance, a causal factor is likely to be poorly performing people and an inordinate amount of time attempting to manage their continued poor performance.

The Wrong People

When I am called in to an under-performing organisation one of the first things the business owner inevitably shares with me is the problems they are having with employees. I frequently hear "my staff are not performing at the level I need them to", "morale is low", "my team need motivating", "my managers are not managing performance effectively" and "there is no buy-in to the growth targets".

A huge amount of time and effort is then put into performance-managing the poorer performers in a way that is compliant with employment law. There is often little return on time invested in this activity as the individuals concerned have little intention to raise their game. In some cases their aim is to do the bare minimum to hang onto their job and collect their salary. Because of the low return on time invested, managers often prioritise other activities over managing performance. A common mistake is for poor performance to be rewarded through continued employment. High-performing companies have no place for payroll passengers.

Do not underestimate the massive shift you will create in your business if you replace 'C class' players with 'A class' players.

Author Jim Collins researched the key variables that make good companies great. He published his findings in the excellent book *Good to Great*. One of his findings was that Good to Great leaders began the transformation by first getting the right people on the bus (and the wrong people off the bus) and then they figured out where to drive it.

If you want to improve your game of golf or your game of tennis, who do you choose to play against? Someone who is at a lower standard than you to ensure you will always beat them or someone who is much better than you who will demand that you raise your game? I suggest the latter is a more effective strategy.

People in the Wrong Seats

Companies large and small often make the mistake of promoting someone into a management role because they were good at the technical role. Being a good engineer, programmer, accountant or sales person does not necessarily mean they will make a good manager or an effective leader.

> *"People are promoted to the level of their incompetence."*
>
> The Peter Principle

Having a square peg in a round hole is not the way to get the best out of someone. In fact, your business is robbed of the time of critical leaders in your business as they manage the sub-standard performance of someone in a role not best suited to them.

"Put your best people on your biggest opportunities, not your biggest problems."

Jim Collins, *Good to Great*

Nature abhors a vacuum. If there is a vacant position there is a rush in many companies to fill that vacancy. The aim, in many cases, appears to get a 'bum on a seat'. The mistaken thinking is that someone in the role is surely better than an empty seat. In the rush to fill the vacancy often the business ends up with the wrong person taking the job – they get themselves A Bum on a seat. I heard one speaker at a conference sum this point up with "It is better to have a hole than an A-hole!"

Inadequate Development of Skills

Within any company, irrespective of size, there is robust competition between different leaders for their slice of a finite training and development budget. In many smaller companies the training and development budget is non-existent because spending money on training and development of employees is not seen as a value add.

Entrepreneurs have often bootstrapped their business. Sheer hard work, common sense and some natural flair have served them well. It is understandable that they would put product development, funding expansion into new markets or a new IT system ahead of paying for training or coaching of key members of staff.

In contrast, people at the top of their game in sport and in the performing arts have received significant training backed up with hours and hours of practice to hone their skill.

If you look at the people in our society who we expect to keep calm and perform at their best during periods of intense pressure: fighter pilots, airline pilots, firemen, armed forces personnel, police, paramedics, doctors and surgeons – they have all had a significant amount of training. Why? Because when it counts we need to be able to rely on them to deliver the goods.

You want your staff to deliver the goods. You

want to 'put the pedal to the metal' and accelerate performance in your business. You will achieve this through your people. Get them to the top of their game. Invest in high quality training and coaching. The return on investment is staggering.

Inadequate Succession Planning

We have spoken about the need to increase the proportion of bright, capable and hungry people in your company. They are essential to accelerate growth.

Part of the package you get with such talent is their desire to move on in their career. Human beings are pre-programmed to seek out challenge and the opportunity to grow. Different people find this in different areas of their lives. For the career / business minded they have an inbuilt desire to progress into new roles, tackle new challenges and, of course, to win. This presents you with an opportunity: what is the next role to provide them for best return? This also requires you to fill their existing role.

I can think of three very different clients I have worked with over the last twelve months. A multinational bank, a £40m owner-managed business and a small business. All had the same problem. They had not addressed the issue of who was going to fill key roles in the business when the incumbent moved on.

Find the talent. Attract them. If not, develop them.

One organisation consistently told me there were not enough good people in the industry. They then took on a bright young Cambridge University graduate. The graduate's new boss told me, before she started: "It will take five years before she will have enough experience of this industry and be adding real value to the business." I suggested he might be pleasantly surprised at how quickly she picked things up and encouraged him to involve her in as much as possible. Five months in he was staggered at how much his protégé had picked up and the value she was adding to the business.

If you have not got the talent in your organisation, recruit for attitude and intellect and nurture the skill and experience.

Tip for the Top

- **Ask a Better Question:**

  "How can we get the right people on the bus and build their capability so we can deliver accelerated growth?"

- **Put your best people on your biggest opportunities**

Chapter 5: Inadequate Capacity (No 'how')

"Give me a lever long enough and a place to stand, and I will move the world."

Archimedes

Current Question a business owner may ask:
"How can I find the time to do this?"

Whether you watch TV programmes such as Dragons' Den or you have watched Business Angels / Investors appraise a potential investment, one key thing you will notice they are looking for is how scalable the business is. Can the business model be replicated in different geographies, in different markets in order to multiply the returns?

Accelerated growth comes through scalability. Businesses that struggle with this have not applied enough leverage within their organisation. Opportunities for leverage can be found with the people in your business, yourself included. A massive goldmine of untapped leverage is people in other companies.

Poor Delegation

The scarcest of all commodities is time. As the business leader, the more you can maximise the return on your time invested, the greater the profitability of your business. When you get everyone in your team thinking about how they maximise the return on their time invested it will turbo boost your company.

People, or specifically human nature, is your biggest challenge with this mistake. When faced with a task that you can do or delegate many will do it themselves, citing reasons such as: "It will take me longer to explain it than to get on and do it myself" or "If you want a job doing properly, do it yourself."

Many hold onto doing the task themselves because they want / need to maintain a sense of control. Their focus should not be on empire building but on delivery of results. Leveraging the time and skill of others is a skill that enables you to multiply your impact. It gives you scalability.

Being busy is not a good measure of a person's success. Busy fools are to be found in every company.

Lack of Efficient Systems

System

Noun: 1. A set of connected things or parts forming a complex whole, in particular.

2. A set of things working together as parts of a mechanism or an interconnecting network.

Clearly the person charged with completing a delegated task needs to know what to do. They can be shown one on one but of course that is time consuming. If you want to roll your product or service out across different geographies you need efficient systems / procedures clearly laid down for people to follow.

I know this sounds like teaching a grandmother to suck eggs but this is where it goes wrong in companies:

Small businesses growth is hampered by a lack of systems. The entrepreneurial business owners would rather invest their time in winning new business than ensuring the correct policy and procedure documentation is written.

In large companies, innovation and flexibility can be stifled by the rigidity of systems. The systems can become overly complex. How many times have you been infuriated by the phrase "The system won't let me" or in the words of Carol Beer, the character in the BBC comedy Little Britain, "Computer says No!"

The McDonald's franchise is a great example of how clear systems have enabled worldwide expansion and ensured the customer experience is the same in Auckland and Anchorage, in Sao Paulo and Seville.

Lack of Leverage of Resource in Other Companies

Many a business leaves money on the table by not tapping into the power of joint ventures.

The thinking in a lot of companies is "We can do this all by ourselves". They think in terms of scarcity, believing if they joined forces with another business on a project that would mean there would be less for them, that they would have a smaller share of a finite pie. Instead, their drive is to beat 'the competition' in order to have it all for themselves.

Working on a project with another business enables you to tap into their people, skills, experience, customer list and technology and them into yours in order to create a win:win.

Tip for the Top

- **Ask a Better Question:**

  "What systems can be put in place to ensure
  this task gets done automatically and
  to the right standard?"

  "Who can I partner with who can help me
  reach more customers whilst benefiting
  them?"

- **Improve your productivity by remembering
  the three Ds: Do it, Delegate it or Dump it**

- **Collaborate rather than Compete**

CHAPTER 6: NO EMBEDDING (NO 'WHEN')

"An organisation's ability to learn, and translate that learning into action rapidly, is the ultimate competitive advantage."

Jack Welch

Current Question a Business Owner may ask:

"What's next?"

"Will this opportunity help the cashflow?"

Changes are not embedded in the company

Addressing the mistakes we have raised so far requires time, energy, expertise. It requires you to change. It requires the people who work with you to change. Embedding changes in a culture is not a tick-box exercise.

Changing our behaviour, changing our habits so they become the norm, so they become the new 'that's how things are done around here' requires consistent reinforcement of the new actions / behaviours until everyone is conditioned.

Given the short attention span of many entrepreneurs, this crucial step is often glazed over in favour of the bright new shiny project coming over the horizon. It is right that you should play to your strengths and turn your attention to the things that will add the most value to your business. Be sure to have someone accountable for embedding the changes into the fabric of your business. Make the changes stick now and last into the future.

Not Saying "No"

"People think focus means saying yes to the thing you've got to focus on. But that's not what it means at all. It means saying no to the hundred other good ideas that there are. You have to pick carefully."

Steve Jobs, Apple

Just in the way that I see many small businesses resisting niching their offering for fear of missing out on opportunity, I see leaders in business struggling with what to say no to. Their thinking can often be short term, asking themselves the question: "Is this opportunity going to help me hit my sales target this year? If so, do it." Busying themselves reacting to the opportunity may increase short-term revenues but often at the expense of following the strategy set.

A friend of mine said that when you say yes to something that is not going to take you closer to your ultimate goal, you are saying no to your goal.

No Plan

We all know the over-quoted phrase "*fail to plan, plan to fail*" and yet it is amazing how many entrepreneurs do not plan. It is in the nature of many to be creative, intuitive and often impulsive. It is being this way that has got them where they are.

There is a time and a place for inspired action and a time for planning out how you are going to implement the strategy in your business that will maximize long-term value and give you the edge.

Another advantage of having a plan is that when the pressure is on and people are feeling it, all they need to do is to look at the plan and take the next step. You will find this will combat any feeling of being overwhelmed.

Take time out to plan or ensure someone in your business takes the time to put together a detailed plan of how you are going to deliver on your strategy.

Not Working the Plan

"Nothing is easier than saying words. Nothing is harder than living them day after day."

Arthur Gordon

It is one thing to plan, it is quite another to work to a plan. Short-term reactionary activities to meet someone else's urgent needs are the enemy of working the plan. Yes, we need to be responsive and have the capacity to deal with the unexpected, but we also need to be disciplined in executing the action plan. It is those with the discipline to follow through that win the prize.

Tip for the Top

- **Ask a Better Question:**

    "Is this opportunity in line with the plan?"
    "Does this opportunity take us closer to our goal?"

- **Work your plan**

In my book *Formula Won for Business*, I take you from No 'How' to 'Know How' by preparing your business for growth. Using my **S C A L E** strategy, we build the capability of your people and your delivery capacity and embed the changes in your business.

Chapter 7: No Legacy
(No 'where next')

"Because the people who are crazy enough to think
they can change the world are the ones who do"

Steve Jobs, Apple

Current Question a Business Owner may ask:

"Things are going well, why should I do anything else?"

Stuck in a Comfort Zone

I have mentioned above that as humans we are pre-programmed for growth. Our default, as in nature, is growth. Where I see entrepreneurs losing their spark is when they get comfortable and they have capable people running their business for them. They enjoy the lifestyle the business is providing them with and spend more time pursuing leisure activities. However, as one retired professional footballer said to me: "There is only so much time you can spend on the golf course." Not that I have anything against golf; my point is the golf can only go so far to meet our human needs (unless you turn pro of course).

"There is always another level."

Gavin Preston

We need challenge and, for many, the sense of contribution. Once the business is up and running, I re-ignite the fire in my clients' bellies by getting them to focus on building a legacy.

No Legacy

We are on the planet for a blink of an eye compared to the life of the planet. I believe that most people would like their lives to have counted for something. This is particularly pertinent for ambitious entrepreneurs.

Business people who are just focused on the money and the lifestyle it provides often see a plateau in their business performance once they have achieved enough income to meet those lifestyle aspirations.

We started off this book highlighting the need for a purpose. Building a legacy; something for you to look back on at the end of your days that you can be proud of, something that will outlive you and leave a positive mark on the planet, takes your purpose to a whole new level.

Constrained by an Old Version of Themselves

Whilst some will have had a passing fantasy about building a legacy, few will make it a reality. They are held back by the version of themselves that kept them operating at the current level. They cannot get past how they see themselves: "Who am I to think that I could make a difference to a nation or across the world?"

There comes a time when we have to get out of our own way. As humans we will often do more for other people than we do for ourselves. Like a snake needing to shed a layer of its skin to grow, we have to be prepared to shed an old version of ourself. If we were to let go of old versions of ourselves, what could we create in their place?

The possibilities are endless, the causes are plenty, and the choice is yours.

Tip for the Top

- **Ask a Better Question:**
  "What do I want my legacy be?"
- **Leave an old version of you behind**

In my book *Formula Won for Business* you'll find my *S T E P* formula to propel you to the next level.

NEXT STEPS

Formula Won for Business

Look out for my next book *Formula Won for Business*. In it, you will get the winning formula for accelerated growth in your business. When you apply the **PACE** formula to your business you may also experience double-digit revenue growth, like a client of mine who took her business from 4.1% growth to 15.6% annual revenue growth in 18 months.

GP Accelerator Weekend

Over three days we roll up our sleeves and get to work applying the *Formula Won for Business* to you and your business. Working with other like-minded entrepreneurs, impatient for better results, we get under the bonnet of your business and develop the strategies to accelerate growth.

Get in touch to find when the next programme is taking place or talk to us about how we can come into your company and get your team in pole position.

You'll find this weekend to be a Game-Changer.

In–House

Gavin and his team can implement *Formula Won in your business*. The focus is on delivering accelerated growth.

www.gavinpreston.com

For the latest blog posts, news and details of the
work we do for SMEs, Corporates and Professional
Advisors.

About the Author

Gavin is passionate about accelerating the performance of entrepreneurial business leaders and their teams. He is known as a 'Game Changer' and the 'Performance Accelerator'. He is sought after across the world by organisations as varied as the United Nations, Aviva, HSBC (Europe and North America), the Egyptian Civil Service, Carphone Warehouse, Ford, BAE Systems and the Institute of Chartered Accountants for England & Wales for his ability to accelerate business / organisational performance and fire up the people within them, often creating double-digit revenue growth as a result.

He has studied human performance for 25 years. He has consulted and coached at the highest level for over a decade. He is a High Performance Coach, a Master Business Practitioner and Master Practitioner of NLP having trained with Dr Richard Bandler and Paul McKenna and served an apprenticeship with NLP Master Trainer Michael Breen. He is a prize-winning KPMG-qualified Chartered Accountant. Gavin is committed to continually raising his game and has invested over £100,000 over the last 20 years in his own development, training with leading experts in their respective fields.

Gavin loves the outdoors and recharges by sailing the waters of Lake Windermere and the west coasts of Wales and Scotland and also by spending time on the hills of the English Lake District and Wales.

Oh, and you may have guessed, he is a big fan of the late Steve Jobs and Apple!

*If you enjoyed this book, found it useful, and
would like a similar one for your own business,
then please contact:*

Kevin Bermingham
kevin@90daybooks.com

www.90daybooks.com